Turn on SAFE POWER
PRINCIPLED CHIROPRACTIC

TO CREATE PROFIT by Design.

Turn on SAFE POWER
PRINCIPLED CHIROPRACTIC to Create Profit by Design

William D. Winship - Dr. Gregory Johnson

Special thanks to

Kathy Ward

for her diligent editing.

"Father says that I'm one little instrument in the great Orchestra of Life, and that I must see to it that I'm always in tune, and don't drag or hit false notes."[1]

---

[1] Porter, Elenor (2013-01-25). Just David (Illustrated) (Kindle Locations 337-338). EirenikosPress. Kindle Edition.

SAFE POWER – PRINCIPLED LEADERSHIP to Create Profit Environments

Copyright © 2015 by **Portacle™**

All rights reserved. This book or any portion thereof may not be reproduced or used in any manner whatsoever without the express written permission of the publisher except for the use of brief quotations in a book review or scholarly journal.

First Printing: 2015

ISBN-13: 978-1519680761

ISBN-10: 1519680767

Portacle™

7057 Mariners Court

Tega Cay, SC 29708

www.portacle.com

www.portacle.com

Dedication 7

Principled Chiropractic - Profit by Design 8

The Covenant - Power of Agreement   10

Stewardship vs. Ownership   12

Leaving a Legacy - Wisdom of Hard Work   24

The Continuous Improvement Model   25

The Improvement Curve   26

Proactively Innovate Instinctively   27

The Math   28

Organize Priorities to Results   30

The Habits 33

Recognize Protocol   35

Think VICTORIOUSLY - Triple Win 37

Articulate - To Understanding   41

Collaborative Trust - Interdependent Actions   44

Least Energy - Remain Sharp   45

Empower SAFE POWER - Mobilize Advancers   46

Metrics to Growth   50

Dedication

We dedicate this book to patients, doctors and the community that the Chiropractic profession serves. May this book give you wisdom and inspiration and understanding.

Experience is the Master Teacher. It is with gratitude in my heart that we point to you - the dedicated professionals - as our real heroes. You are the fearless leaders that have pioneered a movement.

You are the ones shaping healthcare and creating comfort in challenging times.

Even in your frustration, you determine to flourish, and flourish you do.

We dedicate this work to the next generation. You are our real hope - it is your generation that will influence greater futures.

We dedicate this work to the next generation. You are our real hope - it is your generation that will influence greater futures.

portacle.com

Principled Chiropractic - Profit by Design

Our WHY, our HOW and our What!

Why?

We wrote this book in effort to raise the standard in Chiropractic Care, and enhance the health care industry by introducing key ideas that by design will help to build cohesive teams that profit.

In support of that belief we wholly commit ourselves to developing future generations of successful leaders capable of transforming cultures. Dr. Johnson has a vision to be and develop the BEST Chiropractors in the WORLD!

How?

Understanding that Chiropractic care involves business, Dr. Johnson has aligned with Portacle™ and the principles here are based on proven science that develop effective organizational leaders capable of generating healthy and profitable cultures.

What?

We develop effective organizational leaders that understand the principles of passion, trust and character as they relate to transforming the environments in which they live, serve and work.

Portacle™ All Rights Reserved.

This book is a TOOL, filled with concepts and ideas, it is a model to follow as you grow your practice, live your life and help raise the standards of Chiropractic. It is universal in that the principles work in every industry, with every person and will serve to inform and encourage the community who are desirous of improved health, healthcare reform, and genuinely helping others.

On the next page we begin with a *Covenant.* This is a model of the kind of covenant you can create in effort to ensure you remain in alignment with your life journey. This agreement is vital to maintain focus.

The PRIMARY reason a person FAILS, is that they FAIL to FOCUS. Focus produces velocity, and what you focus on generally will materialize.

portacle.com

The Covenant - Power of Agreement

OUR CONFESSION OF FAITH, OUR POSITION IN THE CHRISTIAN COMMUNITY AND MARKETPLACE WE SERVE.

It is our heartfelt desire and determination to serve Christ, our pastors, our employers and all those we encounter in the marketplace and church every day of our lives. We refuse to allow corruption to influence us to do things that do not demonstrate a life of integrity. Our lives are empowered by the Spirit of Almighty God and we make choices to ensure that our position in the marketplace and church is well represented because we are a part of vital teams that are designed to win.

As a matter of integrity, we work to ensure that our leadership is based on leaving a legacy of solutions that produce growth and prosperity for those we serve. We no longer blame the past or the current situations that could have an effect on profitability. We are solution makers looking for innovative ways to leverage time. We are committed to consistently grow relevant skill sets in effort to become more efficient, effective and profitable proving our commitment to excellence.

There are no distractions, or frustrations that we will permit to be in our lives that takes away from the mission and vision for the successful outcome of the impact we have in the church and market place. It is with a missionary zeal we embrace each moment and advance the agenda of the Kingdom of God and the leaders positioned above us whom we are committed to serve. We act as team leaders

Portacle™ All Rights Reserved.

and together our teams make the necessary difference as we influence the culture that creates positive futures for others.

Our position as leaders is a privilege and requires attention to learning and the application of that knowledge in effort to remain qualified and sustain others. We are determined to abandon the gossip and the wrong attitudes that effect our working environment and culture; rather We are working to create a place where others desire to work together for the common goals of the Word of God and as established from others that desire excellence. We realize our voice is heard and because of that influence we are encouraged to cooperate with others to achieve profit by design. We demonstrate exceptionally positive behavior; influence is the fruit of that behavior.

The heart of our effort is to continually prove integrity and establish character based on wisdom from the Word of God which is our life guide book. We have chosen to intentionally live a life of victory that achieves and conquers the enemies that burden growth. We will become dominant influencers that are undeniably focused on life giving attitudes. Our winning and contagious attitude yields regular promotion for us, others and the community at large. As we seek to live this life of authenticity, we choose not receive the glory and recognize that our potentials are simply heaven sent and our responsibility is to mentor and develop others so that those we serve grow in the grace and knowledge of our Lord and Savior Jesus Christ and prosper. I claim victory over every obstacle or challenge. The result of our champion attitude is that others around us enter into the celebration of achievement and become more Christ like.

William Winship October 2, 2007 (edited By Melvin Weaver Dec. 21 2013) Revised to be we centric, September 3, 2015

portacle.com

Stewardship vs. Ownership

Stewardship - the conducting, supervising, or managing of something; especially : the careful and responsible management of something entrusted to one's care.
VS.
Ownership - the state, relation, or fact of being an owner.

This scripture settles for me the Stewardship vs Ownership concerns. Essentially we own nothing but have been entrusted with everything. *"Yours, LORD, is the greatness and the power and the glory and the majesty and the splendor, for everything in heaven and earth is yours. Yours, LORD, is the kingdom; you are exalted as head over all."*

1 Chronicles 29:11

Chiropractic Care is my Passion, it has uniquely challenged my faith and helped me to live a purposeful life. The concept of being a steward opposed to being the owner, is key to being a professional chiropractor.

You might say, it is my "calling" to set the standard of Chiropractic at a level that encourages others to experience the benefits of optimal health.

Early in my life, at the core of my existence a transformational moment forever changed my life.

I was around ten years old when I was diagnosed with Asthma, yet the cause of the trauma had little to do with the diagnosed disorder.

The cause I believe was associated with an accident that occurred prior to the diagnosis. Too often today we treat a disease or disorder without tracing the source that caused the disorder or disease.

I invite you into my youth. As a young man with great energy, like many little boys, I enjoyed vigorous play and loved the thrill of taking risks. If you can imagine me playing on the couch and horsing around with my younger sister. She pushed, I tugged and we fell. The idea of King of the Hill comes to mind. One of us was going to be King. Unfortunately, as I was feeling the power of my strength and enjoying the fun time, I lost my footing. I fell head first, crashing into the solid oak coffee table. Immediately blood was gushing out of my head, and I experienced excruciating pain in my neck and lower back.

My mom immediately held the gushing wound to slow the flow of my gushing head, and took me to the hospital. The blood did slow down, but it required several sutures. As I laid on that gurney, and the doctor stitched me up, I knew that something was missing. Even though the head stopped bleeding, the pain of the event would continue. Pain is a loud reminder that the issue causing the pain has not been restored. Often we try to cover this pain with medication, and when that medication wears off, the pain remains.

In my subconscious mind, I knew that covering over the pain would not resolve the issues. As I laid there I sensed something or someone speaking to me through that pain, and I sensed my purpose emerging. I knew at that moment my assignment on the earth was to deliver people from this kind of pain, yet I had no idea how that would happen.

portacle.com

I believe that the deep love of my mother lead her to a Chiropractor who was schooled at Palmer College of Chiropractic. The experience with this doctor was much different from the one I had at the emergency room. This doctor was more concerned with the damage that was caused to my neck and spine from the impact. It was odd that he was looking at the neck and back to help resolve the Asthma issues. Fundamentally, what does the back and neck have to do with a breathing problem?

According to the National Heart, Lung and Blood Institute, "Asthma (AZ-ma) is a chronic (long-term) lung disease that inflames and narrows the airways. Asthma causes recurring periods of wheezing (a whistling sound when you breathe), chest tightness, shortness of breath, and coughing. The coughing often occurs at night or early in the morning.

At first, I failed to see the correlation between the head injury and my ability to breath in a healthy way. As I learned more things began to make sense. I received "clarity" and began to understand.

The doctor helped me understand my "Calling", I just did not know how great this calling was at the time.

The Chiropractic doctor checked my spine for Subluxations, (Misalignments of the vertebrae causing nerve interference) and he found a vertebrae out of place, (Subluxated) and Adjusted me. He kept aligning my spine to its optimal position and within three months - I had no more asthma, no more allergies, no more medicine, no more allergy shots and no more hospital visits.

I came to value and appreciate this doctor and in Gratitude began a life long journey to be THE BEST CHIROPRACTOR IN THE WORLD.

A passion arose in me and awoke inside of me an innate energy force that compelled me to learn everything I could about the human anatomy and how it operates as God intended. It was as if a light inside of me was ignited and gave me the relentless passion to energize others with this miraculous discovery.

To excel to this measure, "To be the best Chiropractor in the World" I knew it would require discipline, determination and drive. I know internal that this was my life purpose and I better do "Whatever it takes!". To that end I began the journey in martial arts, specifically Tai Kwon Do Chung Do Kwan as a freshman in high school. Fact is, I was a nerdy young man who needed to learn to build focus, self confidence, self discipline, respect and humility. The concept of learning how to break joints may sound a bit counterintuitive to the professional calling, yet it is critical to understand what creates the dysfunction and how to realign things to create harmony often requires that kind of learning. In short, if I could break em, I could mend em.

In addition to understanding the physical cause of misalignment and how to create the alignment it would require more study, and commitment to learning. I began to consume and train my brain in the disciplines of my calling. I read and studied every possible class on human anatomy, biology, chemistry, physics, and human physiology.

This path lead to one obvious place: In my formative years of high school I realized that if I were to be congruent to my calling, it would require the best Chiropractic College in the world. It was with a bit of fear and lots of faith that I applied to Palmer College of Chiropractic in Davenport, Iowa. This school is known for being the Fountainhead of Chiropractic.

The father of Chiropractic D. D. Palmer discovered Chiropractic in 1895 and B. J. Palmer, his son, promoted Chiropractic in effort to become world renowned for the body healing itself when allowed to function without neurological interference.

One of B. J. Palmers brilliant observations is "The Power That Made The Body, Heals The Body". My passion and belief system continued to be shaped as Chiropractic Changed my life, and I gained the understanding of the power of Chiropractic. Admittedly, the medical profession served as an agent to bring me to this awareness and the need of Chiropractic Care for the World. If you need stitches go to the medical doctor, if you need to understand the source of disease, go to a quality Chiropractor.

Much attention is being given to health care with the concept of reforming the medical and health professions, yet we are NOT focused on the solutions. We are spending way too much energy, time and finances on the dysfunctional systems opposed to focused energy on the solution to the problems. This is why this book will give you an advantage, not only in the chiropractic industry but in the practical solutions to join us in changing the world.

The US is almost dead last in the civilized world with our "actual health" and meanwhile the escalation of healthcare continues to climb.

There is something fundamentally very wrong with our healthcare system and the treatment of health that begs for reformation and revival. The solution is no longer to cover the symptoms with toxic drugs and failed medical procedures, but to wake up our civilization to best practices.

Passion, Trust and Character are needed in every profession, and especially in the Chiropractic. Living a principle centered life can be challenging, yet the profession demands that we lead from our professional core. My Purpose in life is to help as many people as I possibly can to understand and receive the benefits of Chiropractic Care.

From the moment of my awakening to the calling of my profession, I have been saying affirmations and writing them down. When you write the vision down, it becomes part of your DNA. In addition to communicating these powerful affirmations, I record and listen to them in effort to ensure that my subconscious and consciousness are in alignment with my practice.

The affirmation that keeps my passion alive is "I Am The Best Chiropractor in the World." This affirmation delivers purpose and helps me to experience the profession with Joy. I sense that the years of leaning, exploring and developing are now very practical. The concept of total integration that include BioPhysics, Bio-Mechanics, Neuropathy Physiology, Neurology, Adjusting Techniques, my innate belief system plus my graduate education at the best Chiropractic College in the world, Palmer College of Chiropractic in Davenport Iowa, have given me the advantage.

portacle.com

Chiropractic Is More Than Just A Job, It's A Life Purpose, Filled With Passion & Trust and Character, of which will demand faith, optimally directed to build a world class practice!

I believe there is a SHIFT in healthcare at the present time. If you are reading this text, it is most likely because you are part of that SHIFT.

People are SICK and TIRED of the political rhetoric, the failed promises and the lack of CURE.

The time has come and NOW is the time where our profession will set the standard to truly impact and help others reach their full potential. This is why this book is so valuable to you. It is filled with wisdom, years of learning and will inspire you to be part of the REVOLUTION in our profession.

People tired of taking pills, potions, shots and surgeries that make them worse in many cases. The human species deserves better care and needs answers to the dysfunctional health care system. We MUST set higher standards and live out of integrity in a world of corruption.

Think about it! Can you put toxins in your body and expect it to heal? This is common sense for most people, yet we have not even begun to shine as a profession.

Putting something foreign in the body or taking something that is supposed to be in the body out of the body is ridiculous when you consider logic.

Portacle™ All Rights Reserved.

Absolutely every organ, muscle, tissue and cell in the human body has a nerve supply and if that nerve supply is interfered with whatever is at the end of that nerve will not function at 100% of that organ's potential. This has been the philosophy of Chiropractic since the beginning of Chiropractic by D.D & B.J Palmer in the late 1800's and early 1900's.

Palmer College of Chiropractic in all three campuses continues to teach this philosophy, science and art. It is this dedication to keep consistent to the cure opposed to covering up that makes our solution so vital. The challenge in any profession, is the dilution of truth, or the failure to operate in that truth, this is precisely why Integrity has to remain the core of the profession.

My bias to Palmer Graduates is simply that the essentials that create health and wellness are driven into the core of the students and the result is that professionals emerge. In addition to our professional understanding is the critical need to understand the "business of the profession", that is where this book becomes useful. The concept of continuous improvement is vital to long term sustainability of our profession and the growth of our message.

The point that I feel is critical is that we remain in a state of pure Chiropractic, opposed to drifting as a profession. Drifting has caused our profession harm, and has confused the patient.

For instance there are some Chiropractic Colleges that do not teach the essential principles that govern high yielding patient experience. Some of these Chiropractic Colleges have been drifting away from the nucleus of true Chiropractic care and in turn implemented schizophrenic methods and ideals such as "Medi-Practor type of Chiropractic Care or therapist, technicians which relies heavily on physical therapy modalities, like E-Stim, hydroculator hot packs, lasers, diathermy, roller tables,(intersegmental traction tables), traction devices, named spinal decompression, ultrasound and other modalities which are not hands on Adjusting and manual therapy using the Chiropractor's hands. In short we are looking outside of pure chiropractic and trying to replace what genuinely works, the laying on of hands. We are designed to be healers, and it is the energy we transmit and the alignment we create with our hands that produces optimization in our patients.

People respond to authentic Chiropractors who lay hands on people and get them functioning and feeling better. A machine will never replace the healing that was authorized by heaven. Jesus himself laid hands on people and healed them of all kinds of illness and disease. It was FAITH, his belief not techniques, machines, lotions or potions that created the cure.

We are there to SERVE people and provide solutions to pain and dysfunction. The idea is to be a professional serving leader that helps the patient to get out of your office and ensure the patients will stay healthy, be glad to pay for the professional services and happily refer others.

Chiropractic Care is about much more than neck pain and back pain, it is about educating your patients to understand the principle that nervous system controls and coordinates the function of every organ, muscle, tissue and cell in the human. Once they understand you care for them and they can trust you then they will receive your help to restore them to optimal life. This kind of care and caring will draw in new patients and ensure your practice continues to THRIVE in a very deprived world. Chiropractic Care is unique, it is a science, philosophy and art of making the body perform the way God intended it to.

Think of it this way, in the womb of your mother, God shaped you. You were created in his image, perfectly. In life, like I experienced, we can be traumatized and our system gets knocked out of alignment. A competent professional Chiropractor will help you to gain back that alignment and help you understand so that you will operate as the one who created you originally determined.

The first system to develop in the embryo is something called the "Primitive Node" which is the brain, the second thing to develop is the "Primitive Streak", the spinal chord which is the Central nervous system then the peripheral nervous system develops which in turn causes our heart to develop, the lungs, the arm, hands, fingers, liver, pancreas, stomach, spleen, kidneys, leg, feet and toes. *Everything in the body has a nerve supply and without it the body will not function properly and we call that Dis-Ease, because when the body is functioning at it's most optimal level it is at Ease.* I.e. Health, (Homeostasis) normal body function, (health).

The world is looking for ways to be healthy. Chiropractic is the secret that needs to be known. Let us together share this secret as we help our patients to be healthy. We can change the world, one patient at a time. The world not only wants to be healthy and it is NOW ready to accept Chiropractic, we have unprecedented opportunity as a profession, and I enlist you in this reformation and revival of Chiropractic. We are professionals and do not put anything foreign into the body or take anything out of the body we just help the body heal itself from within. *"The Power That Made The Body Heals the Body", B. J. Palmer*

I teach other Chiropractors around the world that they can impact people's lives in a very positive way restoring them to optimal health, "EASE" without all the modalities and gimmicks that people don't really benefit from. My hope is that those Chiropractors doing these things will consider "TRUE CHIROPRACTIC" and enjoy the fruit of authenticity opposed to looking for ways to support their practice that are not part of the profession. We need to go back to the basic essentials, opposed to diluting the profession with gimmicks.

Chiropractic Care should begin at birth and go on as a lifestyle. We all need to be adjusted and keep in a state of health. I deeply believe that prevention is so much better than an invasive procedure that can kill the body.

Serve others with skill, and the results will be a happy life, including a happy family and community.

Finally, the GEM of my profession is my amazing assistant and wife Renea. She is more than an assistant, she is my helper, she and I together pray for all our patients, trusting the Lord for direction and wisdom. We are his tool, and place our lives in His hands so that our hands can touch others and and give them life. We understand the real power is that His presence flows through us and that we are his instruments of hope and healing for the world.

"And By His Stripes We Are Healed" Isaiah 53:5

We strive the triple win, "My wife and I win, the Patient and their family become healthy, and the Community built because we Serve the Lord."

Dr. Gregory Johnson, Renae Johnson & Greg Johnson (the Next Generation)

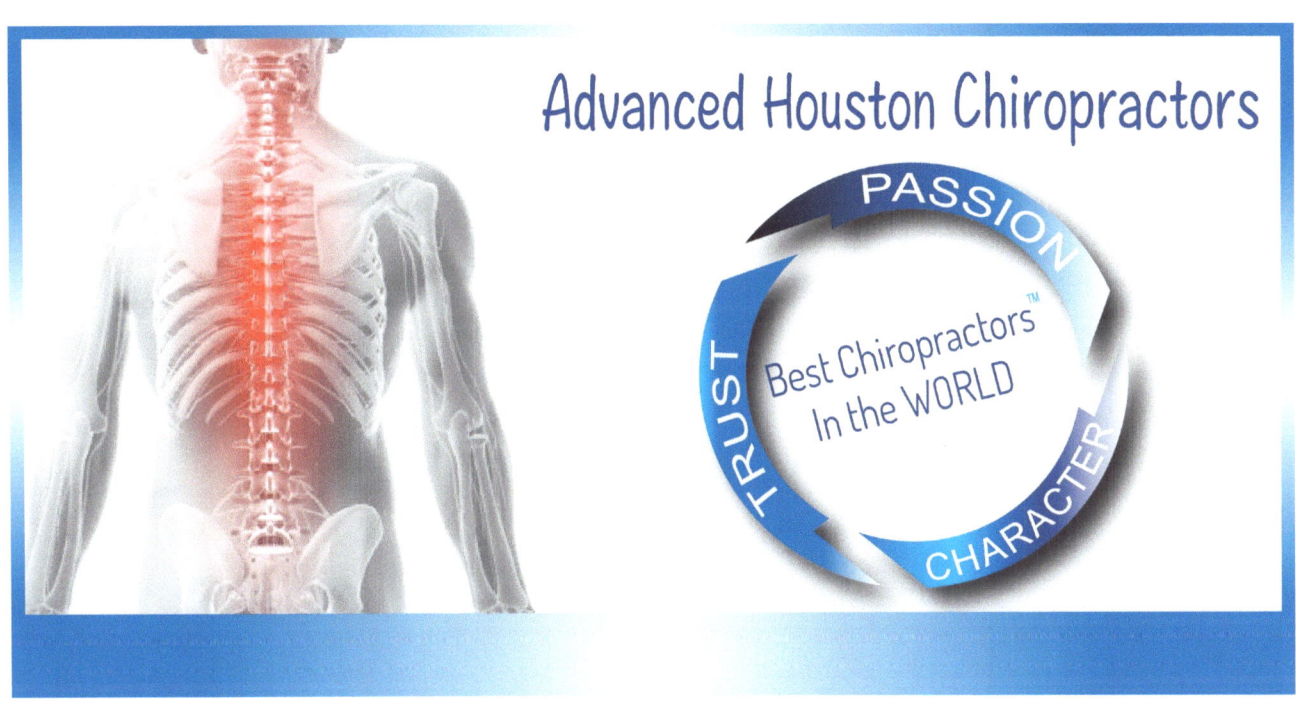

portacle.com

Leaving a Legacy - Wisdom of Hard Work

And Samuel said, Hath the LORD as great delight in burnt offerings and sacrifices, as in obeying the voice of the LORD? Behold, to obey is better than sacrifice, and to hearken than the fat of rams. **1 Samuel 15:22**

You can work very hard, or you can work very smart. Smart people understand that work is worship. We all have flaws, areas where we are not so proud, yet God can use us even if we fail, the best news is that we get a new fresh start every day and if we are wise we make better choices and grow in our faith.

This is the day the Lord has made;
We will rejoice and be glad in it. **Psalm 118:24**

The steadfast love of the Lord never ceases;[a]
    his mercies never come to an end;
they are new every morning;
    great is your faithfulness. **Lamentations 3:22-23**

Life verses:

Observe people who are good at their work—
    skilled workers are always in demand and admired;
    they don't take a backseat to anyone. **Proverbs 22:29 (MSG)**

Never walk away from Wisdom—she guards your life;
    love her—she keeps her eye on you.
Above all and before all, do this: Get Wisdom! **Proverbs 4:7 (MSG)**

Portacle™ All Rights Reserved.

The Continuous Improvement Model

Starting at the bottom, we build trust, master conflict, achieve commitment, embrace accountability and finally focus on results. This process works in a sequence that when applied creates cohesive teams that result in satisfied patients and create profit.

portacle.com

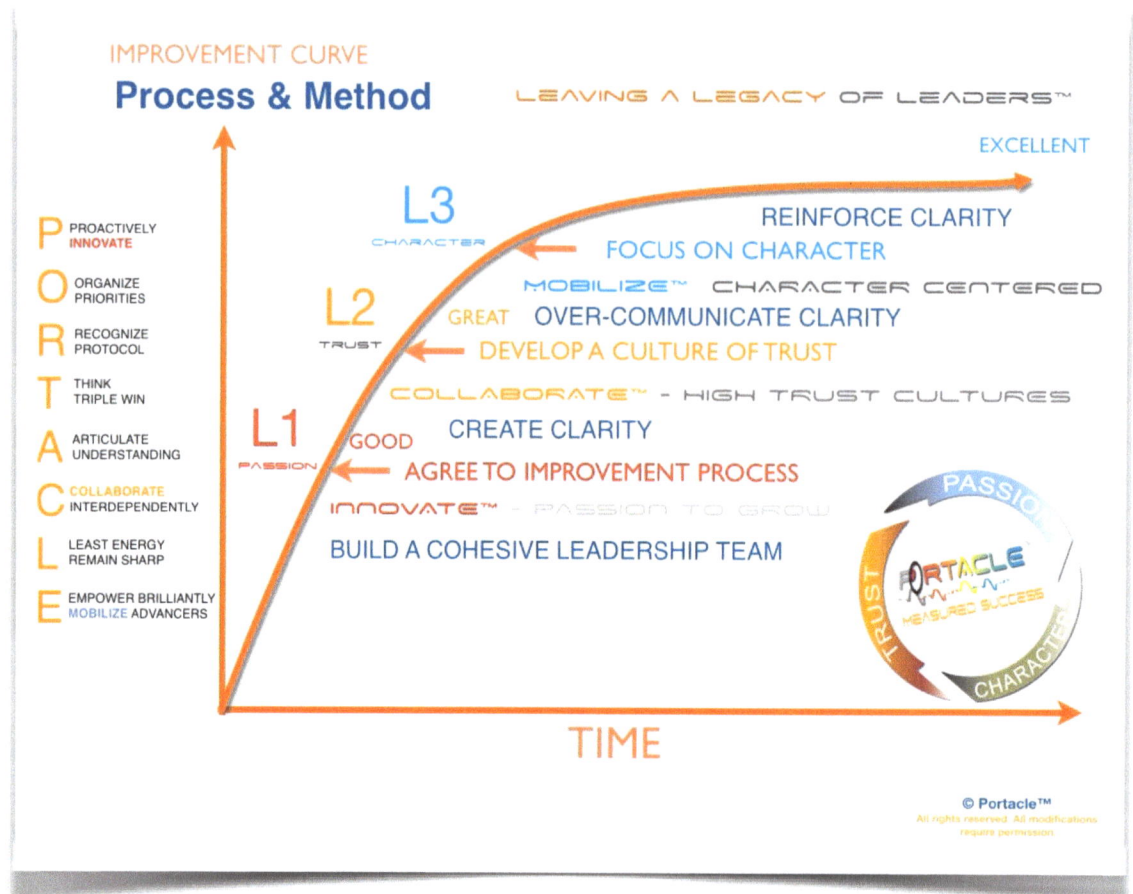

The Improvement Curve

On the left side are principles that govern growth and maturity, in the beginning it is hard work, it takes effort, resources and commitment. The idea is to move from being good, to great, with Excellence being the standard. Having the long term goal of Leaving a Legacy of Leaders, gives you direction. Focus produces velocity, so it is critical to focus with direction.

Portacle™ All Rights Reserved.

Proactively Innovate Instinctively

"Principles of personal vision, you are responsible for change."

Profit is in the Process. Understanding that every business and every organization must be profitable is the key to developing high-yielding cultures that are profitable. In effort to truly be effective, believing that profit needs to exist and that being profitable is a non-negotiable to **organizational HEALTH** and long-term sustainability gives you **the ADVANTAGE!**

Personal responsibility for the professional outcomes of a business and organization is mandatory if you're going to lead.

Growth begins at stage one which is building trust, mastering conflict, achieving commitment, embracing accountability and finally focusing on results.

The Portacle™ virtue orb, specifically incorporates trust, passion and character. We deeply believe that people do business with people they trust, they continue to do business with people of character, and most importantly operate with passion that inspires engagement from others.

Vision that is properly aligned, and communicated helps a business organization to advance.

Many entrepreneurs have certain instincts, and often know exactly what to do, the challenge is that they may not know how to communicate that vision to others so that long-term growth, advancement and fiscal results accumulate.

To proactively innovate means that you take personal responsibility for the innovation of solutions that advance the real mission and vision that governs your growth.

portacle.com

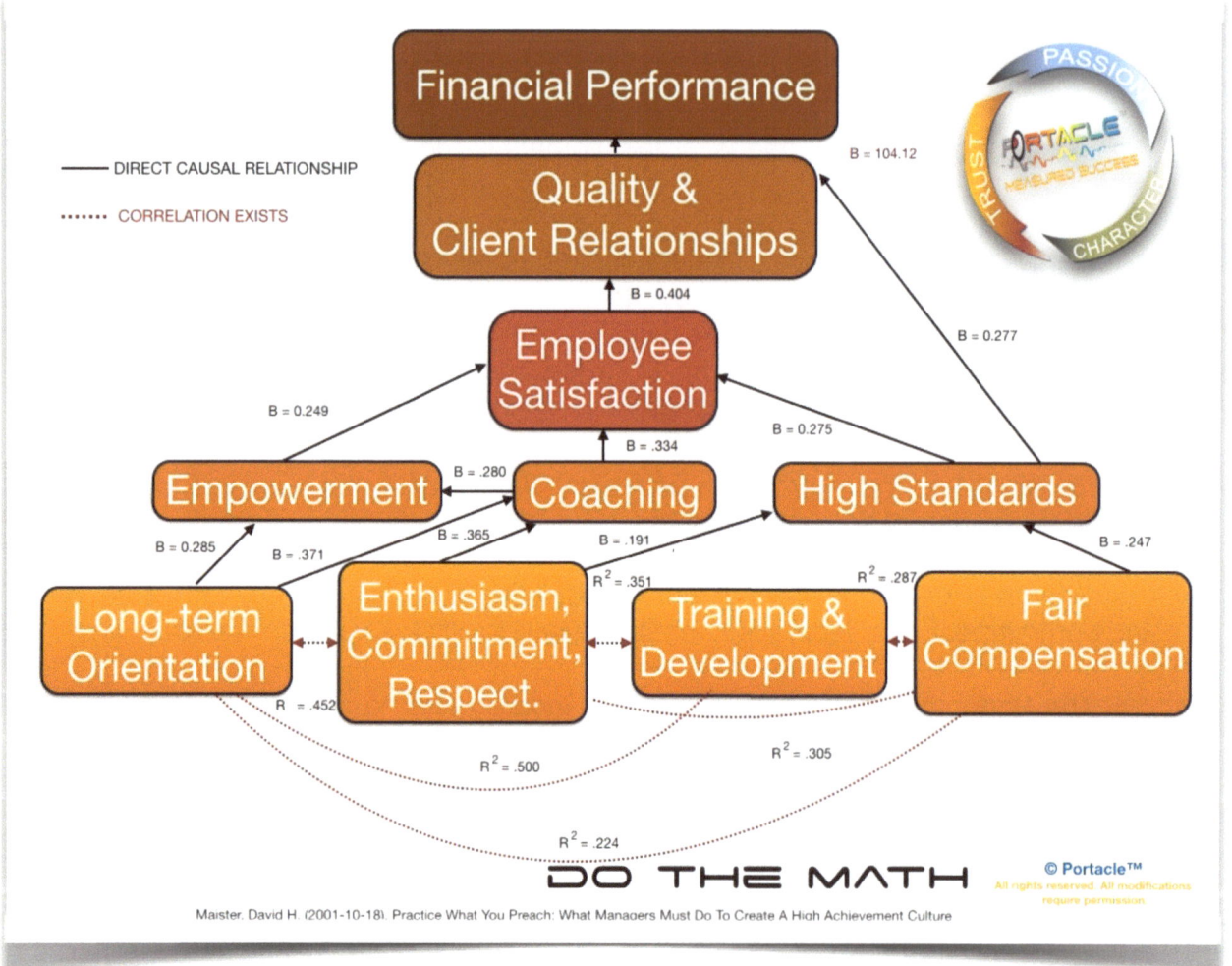

The Math

It is wise to know what creates profit in an organization or business. The diagram above provides that insight. In the book, "Practice what you Preach" David Maister provides this diagram. The science of this diagram is based on surveying organizational cultures to determine how to create cultures that perform financially or **Profit by Design.**

Portacle™ All Rights Reserved.

Proactively *Innovate* (Vision)
-Principles of personal vision, you are responsible for change.

How do you form vision?

How do you share vision?

How do you know if others are buying into the vision?

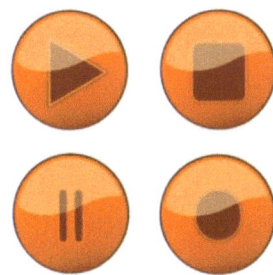

© Portacle™
All rights reserved. All modifications require permission

portacle.com

Organize Priorities to Results

"Aligning Passion Priorities - imagination of greater futures, and creating fresh scripts for life."

This principle is about keying into an organized profitable movement, and not allowing past events to hinder forward progression. Ensuring that you employ systems, controls and established incentives that are in place as you execute the agreed to mission, remain focused on a shared vision and engineer the cohesive team. Understanding the real passion of the organization and aligning that organization to measured results gives you an edge. This principle does not settle for mediocrity, instead it is set to higher standards that provide for higher engagement. **Profit by Design**, includes the total intellectual contributions of the entire team.

It is imperative to identify the key dysfunctions in a team. In the book, "Five Dysfunctions of a Team", Patrick Lencioni articulates those dysfunctions.

The assumption that this principle assumes is that most people do not want to have a dysfunctional organization or business. Knowing the key dysfunctions helps to identify the solutions to those dysfunctions. Once known, we focus on clarity. We must be very clear on the things we need to change in order to have effective results.

This principle ensures that we focus on the development of a cohesive team that is aligned to **Profit by Design.**

Portacle™ All Rights Reserved.

Foundational to profit is to identify the dysfunctions, eradicate those dysfunctions and build a high-yielding culture. Knowing what creates dysfunction helps us to understand that which creates harmony. Harmony, is intentional and requires an orchestra of leaders working together toward higher achievement.

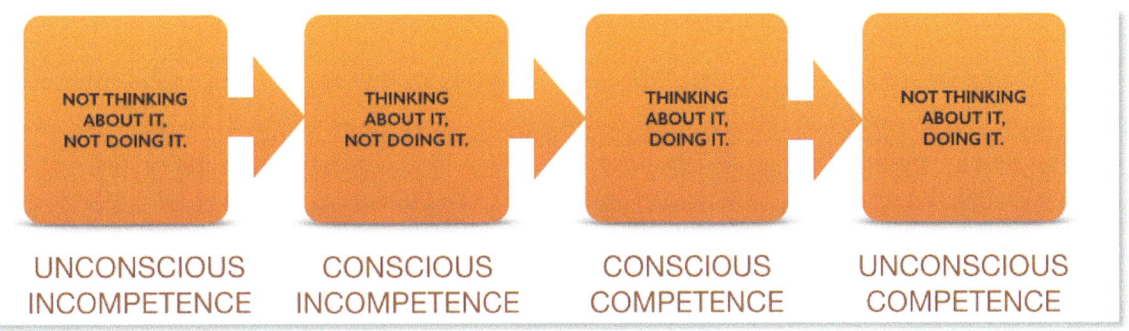

Dysfunction #1: Absence of Trust: Members of great teams trust one another on a fundamental, emotional level, and they are comfortable being vulnerable with each other about their weaknesses, mistakes, fears, and behaviors. They get to a point where they can be completely open with one another, without filters. This is essential because . . .

Dysfunction #2: Fear of Conflict: . . . teams that trust one another are not afraid to engage in passionate dialogue around issues and decisions that are key to the organization's success. They do not hesitate to disagree with, challenge, and question one another, all in the spirit of finding the best answers, discovering the truth, and making great decisions. This is important because . . .

portacle.com

Dysfunction #3: Lack of Commitment . . . teams that engage in unfiltered conflict are able to achieve genuine buy-in around important decisions, even when various members of the team initially disagree. That's because they ensure that all opinions and ideas are put on the table and considered, giving confidence to team members that no stone has been left unturned. This is critical because . . .

Dysfunction #4: Avoidance of Accountability: . . . teams that commit to decisions and standards of performance do not hesitate to hold one another accountable for adhering to those decisions and standards. What is more, they don't rely on the team leader as the primary source of accountability, they go directly to their peers. This matters because . . .

Dysfunction #5: Inattention to Results: . . . teams that trust one another, engage in conflict, commit to decisions, and hold one another accountable are very likely to set aside their individual needs and agendas and focus almost exclusively on what is best for the team. They do not give in to the temptation to place their departments, career aspirations, or ego-driven status ahead of the collective results that define team success.[2]

---

[2] Lencioni, Patrick M. (2007-07-23). Overcoming the Five Dysfunctions of a Team: A Field Guide for Leaders, Managers, and Facilitators (J-B Lencioni Series) (p. 8). Wiley. Kindle Edition.

Portacle™ All Rights Reserved.

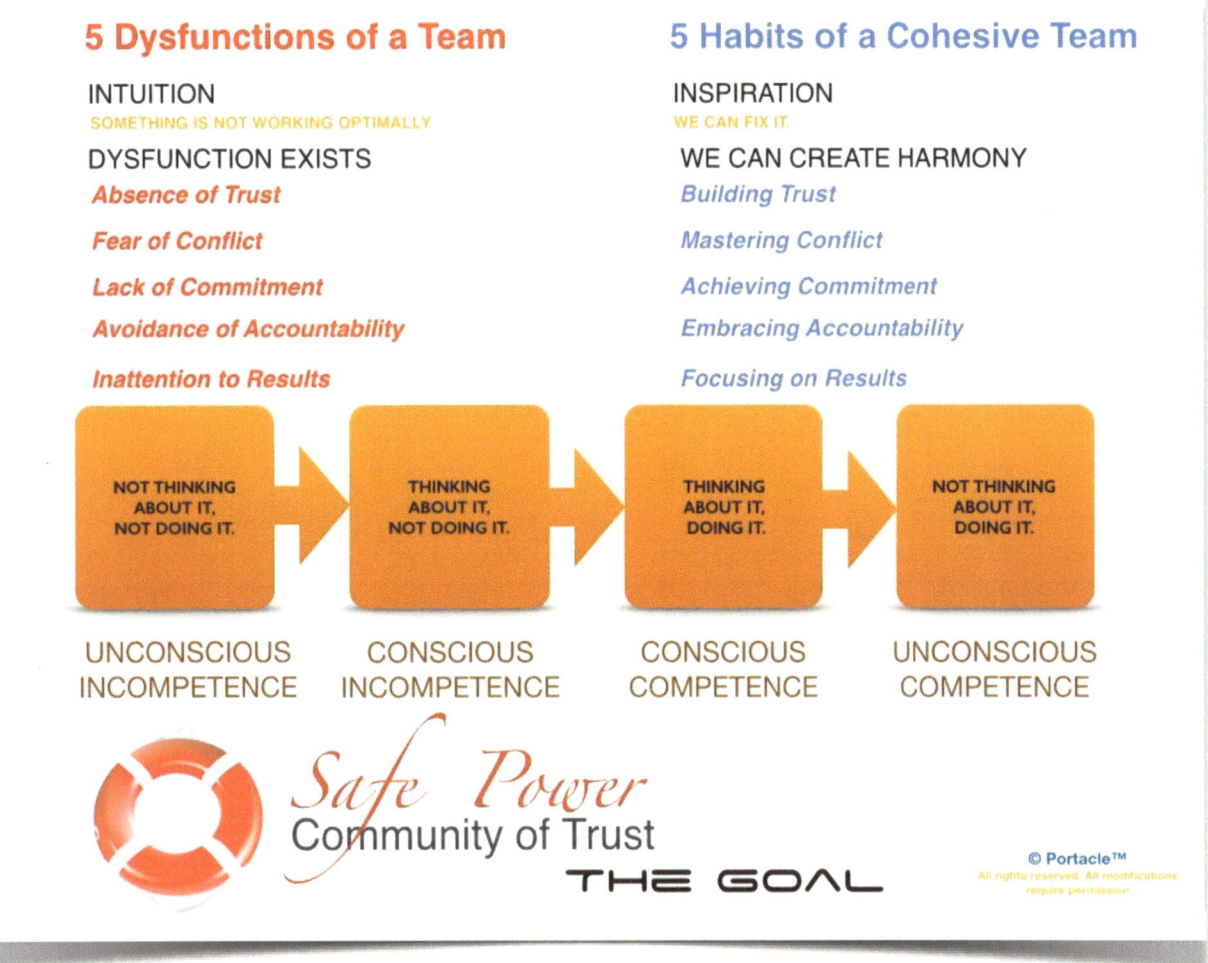

The Habits

Habits create futures, unfortunately if we are not careful we can form BAD habits opposes to those that serve a brighter future. On the left side we understand the problems that exist in dysfunctional teams, on the right we gain insight on what creates healthy and prosperous futures.

portacle.com

Organize Priorities to Results (Strategy/Plan)
-Aligning achievement through imagination of great futures, creating new scripts in life.

How do you develop strategy?

How do you share strategy with others?

How do you change the narrative of a culture?

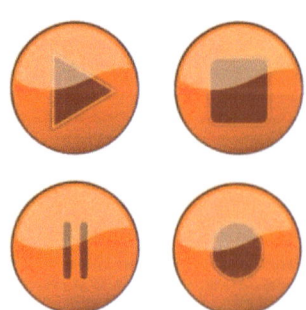

© Portacle™
All rights reserved. All modifications require permission.

Recognize Protocol

"Advance with discipline and model serving leadership that operates with authority and honors protocol at all times."

Perhaps the number one reason that an organization fails is that someone within that organization and throughout the rank-and-file breaks protocol.

If the point of the organization is to be profitable, then those cooperating with a profit centered culture will need to have clear understandings of their roles and responsibilities as they contribute to the cohesive team. Failure to articulate a clear understanding produces frustration and confusion and ends in revenue loss.

Let us consider the airline industry as an example. If you can imagine, in order to keep an airline running there are many parts and pieces that must be assembled in order to create safe travel. As a passenger, my role is to ensure that I have paid for my ticket, have the proper identification and follow the mandatory requirements so that I can qualify to fly.

If I were to get on the airplane, decide to sit in the cockpit rather than my assigned seating - it is likely that I will be greeted by a federal air marshal and ushered off the aircraft.

The point I am making is that protocol is needed in order to provide order and safety in any business or organization.

portacle.com

Recognize Protocol (Team Engagement)

-Advance with discipline and model serving leadership that operates with authority and honors protocol at all times.

Why is protocol important?

How do you model serving leadership?

How do you define authority?

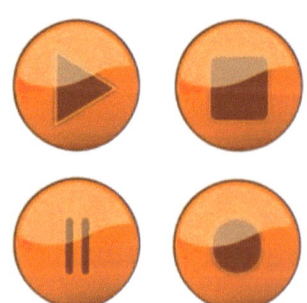

© Portacle™
All rights reserved. All modifications require permission.

Think VICTORIOUSLY - Triple Win

"Living authentically so that the long view is established. Form agreements based on serving, empowering others to serve, and Influencing those you serve with results they need."

Authenticity is a term that would indicate integrity and character exists within a person and personality of a corporate culture. The fact is many businesses have been operating in absence of true character and lacking integrity. It is interesting for me as a business consultant to watch organizations and businesses fail simply because they have not organized their human capital. Many companies today have a very limited view of a real mission that drives the corporation to perform with excellence. Short of doing what I would call "heavy lifting" and organizing a business around the genetics of authenticity, survival is the norm. When we communicate around the concept of thriving in the present culture, that means we have to do things differently. To be optimal and have a competitive advantage, **it requires work.**

Coercion and manipulation have been the tools used to provoke sales in many businesses and organizations, sadly those tactics only produce short-term gains. Authenticity considers the longview, it considers things like the triple win. In the not so distant past, it used to be good enough to have a win-win.

Here's an example of a win-win: You enter into a car dealership for the purpose of purchasing an automobile. You find the most amazing automobile and decide to purchase it. Even after you make your decision you hear the salesman use old tricks, and try to spin the conversation, yet you overlook those things because you want the car. The salesman is nice and helps facilitate the deal, and he may even genuinely appear to care about you. It appears as you leave the car dealership you win - because you were able to purchase the car of your dreams, and the salesperson wins because he receives his commission. I call that a transaction, opposed to a negotiation because anyone can go to a gum ball machine and buy a gum ball. The fact is, you might not even remember the sales person's name or ever recommended him or her to anyone because it just isn't that important.

    Here's an example of a triple win. You go into the same car dealership and you find the car of your dreams. This time you don't meet a salesman, but someone who is negotiating for your best interests. You see the car that you think you want to buy, and the negotiator (opposed to a cheesy sales person) evaluates specifically what it is that you want, and determines that the car you think you were going to buy falls short in a few areas. Instead of spinning you into a deal, he requests a few days to do some research to find the car that is more suitable for you and has greater value. You agree, and he calls you after diligently researching and suggests a car at another dealership. He has located an automobile with all the options that you were hoping for, and forgoes his commission. This behavior shocks you. Five years later you discover that same negotiator that helped you now owns the dealership, and is the most trusted car dealership in the city.   It was perplexing to you that he would forgo a sale. The epiphany hits you, and it becomes clear that this highly skilled negotiator was just acting out of the spirit of authenticity, and his character over the years rewarded him with the best car dealership. The negotiator understood the difference between a transaction and building a long-term future.

Triple wins promoted the negotiator and those he serves.

portacle.com

Think - Triple Win (Resource)

-Living authentically so that the long view is established. Form agreements based on serving, empowering others to serve, and influencing those you serve with results they need.

Why is a longview important?

Define a triple win?

How do healthy agreements improve performance?

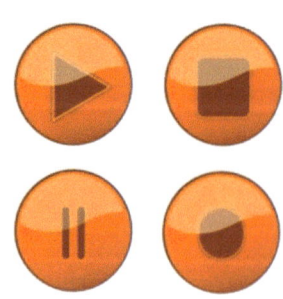

© Portacle™
All rights reserved. All modifications require permission.

Articulate - To Understanding

"Listen deeply to understand the needs, desires and goals of others, then align your persuasion with integrity to achieve optimal relational excellence and team growth."

When you listen from the heart to genuinely hear and appreciate another person - you position yourself to understand. Steven Covey said, in the "Seven Habits of Highly Effective People", that we are to listen in order to understand. In Proverbs 4:7 in the Bible, it says; ***Wisdom is the principal thing, therefore get wisdom, with all thy getting get understanding.***

Listening from the heart to genuinely understand is a gift. Listening is a skill, that when coupled with your ability to communicate helps to ensure alignment. When you listen deeply to understand, you will then articulate more clearly and your voice will be heard.

There are many times in our "relational excellence" course where a couple hears each other for the very first time.

Hearing words, is not the same as hearing the essence of that individual. To truly hear, is to tune into that other person and get to know and understand them.

I remember some years ago, meeting a young man at a conference. Ryan was a brilliant, inspiring young man who had much to offer humanity. He was the product of a divorced home and felt that his life was worthless.   I remember entering into his world, and discovering

portacle.com

that he was 'dumbing' down his intelligence with narcotics. Ryan had essentially lost all hope, and was ready to commit suicide.

After days of discussion, he gained a new hope and decided that his life truly mattered. He and his father were reunited, and they resolved years of conflict. This young man then joined the family business, and moved up in the rank-and-file to lead the business as a next-generation owner.

Sadly, one evening he fell asleep at the wheel, crossed the yellow line and died instantly in a head on collision. His father called me and let me know that on his night stand he found the book that I had signed and dedicated to Ryan.

Ryan was an over-comer, a young man who died too early, but made a significant difference in every life he connected with.

The point is, that once he understood his purpose he did the greater things, and the greater things are to influence positive change.

Another example is, a client who had a daughter that was involved in a lesbian relationship. This young girl, really never understood or knew her father. In our conversation she agreed that my wife and I could adopt her as her temporary parents. I remember looking in her eyes, letting her know that it was okay that she had experimented sexually, and that she was a heterosexual. She believed, and in that moment changed her life. She is now married to the man of her dreams and they are planning their family together.

Articulate - To Understanding (Execute)

-Listen deeply to understand the needs, desires and goals of others, then align your persuasion with integrity to achieve optimal relational excellence and team growth.

Why is understanding curtail to conversations?

How well do you know your team?

Do you articulate your needs and goals so others buy in?

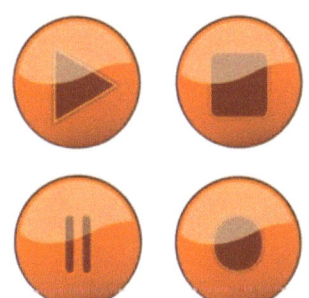

© Portacle™
All rights reserved. All modifications require permission.

portacle.com

Collaborative Trust - Interdependent Actions

"Creative cooperation, ensuring that the total intellectual, emotional and passions of the team are understood before taking any actions."

Cohesive teams are built through an accelerated Learning environment, keying in on eight vital learnings. Below you will see a blueprint where we dissect these trainings into the four quadrants, creating a total integration of knowledge and skills needed to be optimal as an organizational leader, and on a personal level.

Collaborate - Interdependent Action (Measure)
-Creative cooperation, ensuring that the total intellectual, emotional and passions of the team are understood before taking any actions.

Why is collaborating so hard?

What needs to exist to be interdependent?

Why is it important to gain contributions before executing?

© Portacle™
All rights reserved. All modifications require permission.

Least Energy - Remain Sharp

"Key in on continuous improvement both personally and professionally. Remaining in a state of continuous improvement and developing high performance, requires that you remain diligent to excellence as the standard."

Below is a path that we follow, including the process that involves metrics. **What you don't measure and understand might be the difference between having a competitive advantage, or losing market share.**

Least Energy - Remain Sharp (Refinement)
-Key in on continuous improvement both personally and professionally. Remaining in a state of continuous improvement and developing high performance, requires that you remain diligent excellence as the standard.

Why is EXCELLENCE the standard?

How can you be more efficient?

What happens when continuous improvement stops?

© Portacle™

Empower SAFE POWER - Mobilize Advancers

"Long view considerations that produce results. Leaving a Legacy of Leadership™"

Leaders or leadership can be very confusing. I suggest that everyone is a leader. The challenge is that not all leaders have the DNA to achieve the highest ideal. A case can be made for a lack of Character. If Character is the DNA of a person and of an organization you will clearly hear evidence throughout the rank and file.

The conversations will be authentic and promotion typically becomes the team victories that serve others genuinely. The winning culture will aspire to excellence, be engineered around the total intellectual contributions of others and exhibit behaviors that are tuned into integrity, and execute authentically. **Congruency occurs the moment when people align with proven principles and we can observe behaviors that provide Profit by Design.** The modeling of these behaviors is best practice and serve to govern the decisions of those serving. Adherence to absolute process discipline will help as the work is being performed. *It is especially important at the top of the organization to remind yourself, that you are ONE, and one little instrument, in a greater Orchestra, when it becomes about YOU and not the whole, you have drifted way off course.* **If YOU are not committed to excellence, FORGET IT.** Change is Personal, like leadership. Leadership that effects change is always turning into progress because **"Profit is in the Process"**.

Portacle™ All Rights Reserved.

As an example, in a high yielding and committed culture you would not hear a member blaming, justifying or defending bogus actions, but rather they would have permission to fail, and share and learn from the mistakes that are certain to happen. Maturity sounds much different and produces higher yields for all concerned. What you would hear in a maturing culture are people that have a commitment to innovate better solutions, possess compassion with a genuine curiosity to collaborate with the team and understand their end game which is to mobilize others to excellence.

Serving leaders that inspire growth genuinely hold the keys to continued improvement and sustainable futures. Essentially this kind of leader considers the eternal future and impact of their decisions and actions, with an eye on best practice. These leaders are master communicators who model greatness, with their first priority being to take personal responsibility for their actions and activities. Three attributes that are normally present in their interactions with others are clarity of mission, compassion for others, and a genuine curiosity to learn and set a higher standard and have a commitment to excellence.

Empathy for future generations is at the heart of those who "Leave a Legacy of Leaders™". It is their considerations of futures and their leadership that governs the entity to perform with Safe Power, and to develop **Profit by Design**. These leaders instinctively know that a well governed entity that is profitable is the ideal.

Attentive serving leaders stay the course by continuing to sharpen their skill to ensure that competence and character are in balance. These leaders understand the importance of the triple win. They negotiate with a clear end in mind that serves future generations. These kinds of leaders are principle centered and empower great behavior and give great advantage to everyone they serve. They ultimately have a generous desire to see the emergence of passion in others.

Those who "Leave a Legacy of Leaders™" own the Portacle™ Virtue Orb and have installed the attributes into their DNA. These leaders weigh actions and decisions around integrity and possess the Character to generously invest in the next generation, and have the authenticity needed to establish Trust and diligently operate with a missionary zeal to ensure the Passion of the entity is carried out.

Those who "Leave a Legacy of Leaders™" will one day fade away, but the substance of what they leave behind will be positively contagious and produce profit environments that last for generations.

You don't need any of their so-called teaching. Christ's anointing teaches you the truth on everything you need to know about yourself and him, uncontaminated by a single lie. Live deeply in what you were taught. 1 John 2:18-27 MSG

My assumption: *"You know what to do."*

My advice: **Just do it.**

Empower SAFE POWER - *Mobilize* Advancers (Sustain & Grow)
-Long view considerations that produce results. Leaving a Legacy of Leadership™

Who are advancers?

How can you be an advancer?

Why are advancers needed?

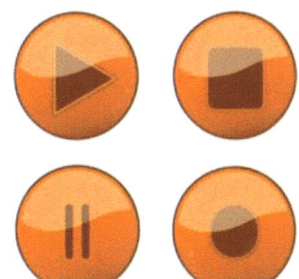

© Portacle™
All rights reserved. All modifications require permission.

portacle.com

Metrics to Growth

An old saying, "You cannot manage what you do not measure", is somewhat applicable to developing long term profit. On the maturity curve is a sequence of tools we use to help develop and advance people to operate at a level optimization.

Portacle™ All Rights Reserved.

Smart & Healthy
2 REQUIREMENTS FOR *COMPETITIVE ADVANTAGE*

Strategy

Marketing

Finance

Technology

Minimal Politics

Minimal Confusion

High Morale

High Productivity

Low Turnover

Lencioni, Patrick M. (2012-03-14). The Advantage: Why Organizational Health Trumps Everything Else In Business (J-B Lencioni Series) (p. 11). Wiley. Kindle Edition.

© Portacle™
All rights reserved. All modifications require permission.

"The Competitive Advantage, be practical and healthy."

The BASIC tenants of business.
What are your strengths, weakness, opportunities, and threats?
What is your Vision?
Is it aligned with your Mission?
What are your Core Values, the NON negotiable?
What are your personal and professional Goals?
What gives you the edge, what are you doing to have the Competitive Advantage?

For more worksheets:
http://portacle.com/36-resources.html

Portacle™ All Rights Reserved.

Worksheet #1
SWOT Analysis

Review your company. In that review, identify any strengths, weaknesses, opportunities, or threats that may impact your ability to effectively compete. Add more points as necessary—don't limit the answers only to the 4 shown.

My Company's strengths are:

1.

2.

3.

4.

My Company's weaknesses are:

1.

2.

3.

4.

The external opportunities that exist for my Company include:

1.

2.

3.

4.

The external threats that may impact my Company include:

1.

2.

3.

4.

Date completed: _____ Your Name: _____

© Portacle™
All rights reserved. All modifications require permission.

**Worksheet #2
Core Values**

Core values are those who you want to build the Company around. List these in any order, and then go back and assign a Rating to each one, with 1= Highest Importance to 10 = Lowest Importance. Don't try and list them all in one sitting, take your time and do this exercise over a period of time so that you can determine all that will be the root basis of what you are creating. Add more points as necessary; do not limit yourself to just 10 if you have more.

Rating	Desired Core Values
_____	1.
_____	2.
_____	3.
_____	4.
_____	5.
_____	6.
_____	7.
_____	8.
_____	9.
_____	10.

Date completed: _____   Your Name: _____

© Portacle™
All rights reserved. All modifications require permission.

Worksheet # 3
Company Goals

In order to foster growth of my Company, and realize the dreams I have for it, these quantitative and qualitative goals are foremost in my mind. List all that come to mind, even if seem minor at this point. Do not limit the number to 5 each, add as many as come to your mind. Establish a target date for achieving each goal, but do not spend too much time determining each date as changes may be forth-coming or reasons will become evident to make changes, as we continue through this Planning Program.

My Quantitative Goals with corresponding Target Dates are:

1.

2.

3.

4.

5.

My Qualitative Goals with corresponding Target Dates are:

1.

2.

3.

4.

5.

Date Completed: _____   Your Name: _____

© Portacle™
All rights reserved. All modifications require permission.

portacle.com

Worksheet # 4
Vision Statement

A Vision is not necessary to create and operate a successful company; however, if one doesn't understand why he/she started this business, it may be difficult to formulate a plan for going forward. If you don't have a Vision Statement for your Company now, we strongly recommend developing one. Developing a Vision and applying it creates a strong community of colleagues, customers, friends, employees, and partners. If everyone doesn't buy into your Vision, don't despair or worry, because it is human nature to not always agree. Just go for it.

Think Big! Be unreasonable! Be willing to be scoffed at! Just identify the end, make it bright enough to light the path to success.

Remember, a vision is not a map of how your dream will be accomplished. Rather, it is a short phrase that serves, not proves. That is left for the Mission Statement, on the next Worksheet. To get you started, here is an example of a very successful company's Vision: *"To Deliver The Next Day."* Can you guess the name of the Company?

Now list as many ideas you can think of as the Vision for your Company. Don't limit the number, just let it flow. We'll pare it down later!

1.
2.
3.
4.
5.
6.
7.
8.
9.
10.

© Portacle™
All rights reserved. All modifications require permission.

Worksheet # 5
Mission Statement

The mission statement follows after the Vision Statement, because it is the road map of How. It is a way to share who you are, why you are doing this, and to continuously remind you and everyone around you what your purpose is.

Here are several steps you need to consider before formulating ideas for your Mission Statement:
1. List the important products or services your Company offers of which you are most proud.
2. Why are you proud? List these, be very specific.
3. If every appropriate person in the world had access to these products or services, what difference would that make to civilization? To each person?
4. Without access to your product or service, how do people suffer or what opportunities do they miss out on?
5. If you had the resources, what single product or service would you spend your life making sure as many people as possible had access to?
6. Why do you care so much about this product or service?

Now write down as many versions of your Mission as you can. Don't limit your ideas right away. We'll pare this down later. Eventually, strive for the three that fit your plan the best. We'll find the Mission Statement out of those best three!

1.

2.

3.

4.

5.

6.

7.

8.

Date Completed: _____   Your Name: _____

© Portacle™
All rights reserved. All modifications require permission.

portacle.com

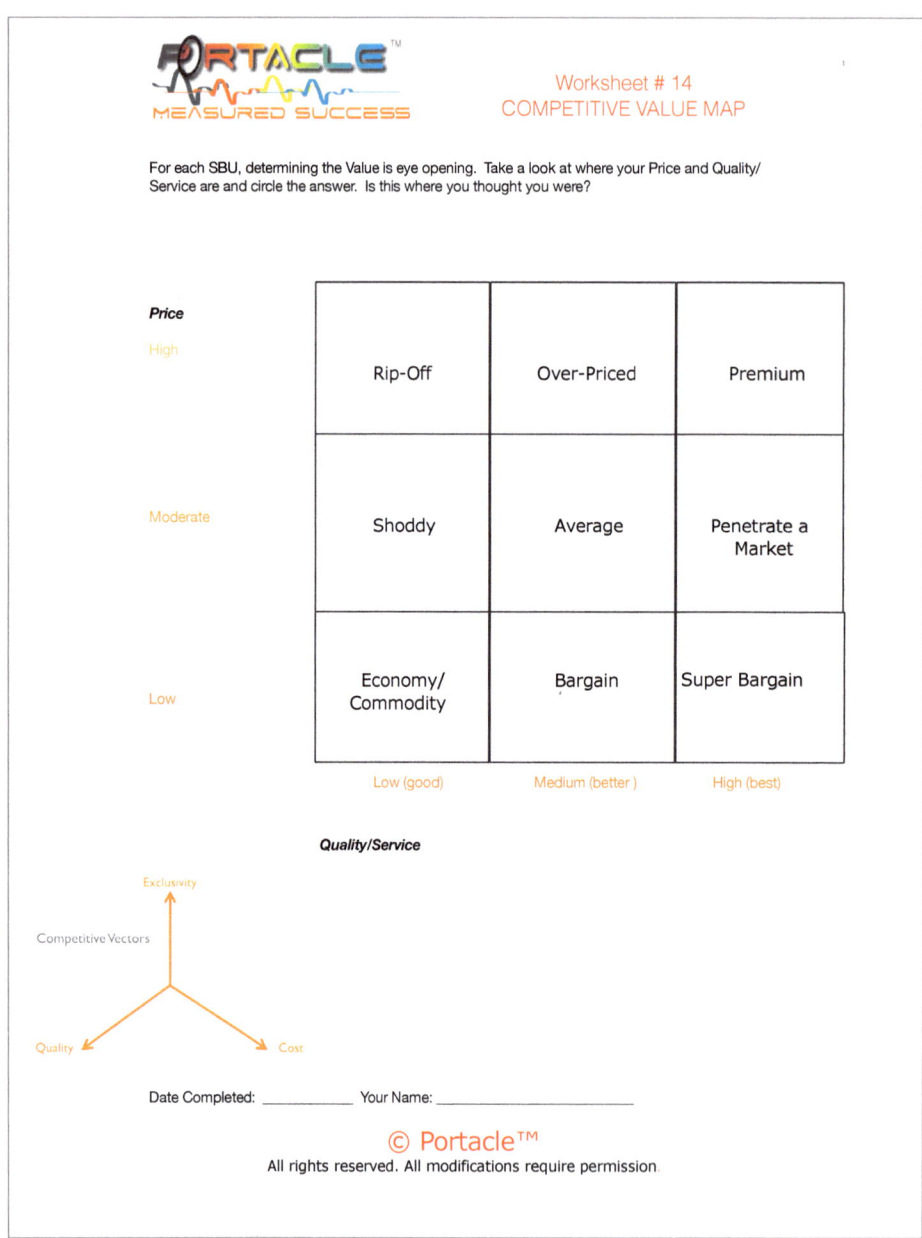

www.ingramcontent.com/pod-product-compliance
Lightning Source LLC
Chambersburg PA
CBHW051050180526
45172CB00002B/579